LUDLOW FOOD HEROES
IN SUPPORT OF
HELP FOR HEROES

BY DAVID CAREY

First Published 2012
Published by Templar Books
Copyright © Templar Books 2012

David Carey has asserted his right under the Copyright,
Design and Patents Act, 1988, to be identified as the
author of this work.

ISBN: 978-1-909378-00-1

Printed by Orphans Press
Leominster Enterprise Park
Leominster
Herefordshire
HR6 0LD

TEMPLAR MEDICAL IS PROUD TO SPONSOR

LUDLOW FOOD HEROES
IN SUPPORT OF
HELP FOR HEROES

TEMPLAR MEDICAL LTD

PROVIDER OF BESPOKE HEALTH AND MEDICAL SERVICES

WWW.TEMPLARMEDICAL.CO.UK

CONTENTS

PREFACE

I first joined the military in 1986 as a pilot with the Royal Navy's Fleet Air Arm. Since then I flew commercially and then retrained as a doctor. Firstly as a surgeon with the British Army and then transferring back to the Royal Navy as a consultant in military operational medicine with a subspeciality in Aviation & Diving Medicine. Since 1986 I have seen many changes both within the military and more recently within military medicine and the management of military patients.

The advances in care for military personnel are matched only by the demands placed upon them. In 1986 we were confined predominantly to the Cold War but since then the diversity and tempo of operations has increased beyond imagination. Sailors, soldiers and airmen can now find themselves deployed on operations in roles they previously would not have imagined. Army pilots may find themselves embarked on naval carriers, whilst naval mine clearance divers carry out Explosive Ordnance Disposal (EOD) on foot patrols in Afghanistan, whilst air force or navy medics occupy Forward Operating Bases (FOBs) alongside Army infantry or Royal Marine commando units.

By sharp contrast the dedication of our troops has changed very little. Sadly, nor has the cost in terms of human life and suffering. Most of us know someone serving however the close relationship between regiments, squadrons and ships and the communities they recruit from is not as clear as it once was. In 2012 I leave the military and I wanted to create a modest book that did nothing more than forge a connection between a local community and the military.

Accordingly, this book is just one small contribution from the people of Ludlow and the surrounding area to show their appreciation of the sacrifices made, both past and present, by our service personnel.

David Carey MSc MB BS MFOM DAvMed MRAeS
Surgeon Commander, RN

FORWARD

A s I sit out here writing this, in forward operating base Ouellette in Afghanistan thoughts of England are never far away.

I was last in Helmand Province in 2009 as part of The Light Dragoon battle group. Towards the end of the day on 4th July while involved in Operation Panther's Claw my troop came under heavy and sustained fire from an enemy ambush point. The contact resulted in the loss of one of my soldiers, Private Robbie Laws, and the amputation of my right leg below the knee – the effects of a rocket propelled grenade piercing the hull of my vehicle.

At the time Help for Heroes was still a relatively new charity, however all of the soldiers I worked with in Afghanistan were fully aware of the great work it was doing. Once back to the UK and into the throws of rehabilitation at Headley Court I continued to see the incredible work it was doing first hand.

Two years later I was lucky enough to be part of an expedition which sought to achieve a world first, by putting war wounded soldiers on the geographic North Pole trekking completely unsupported. We had two main goals; firstly to fundraise for the re-education and re-training of wounded servicemen and women and secondly to raise awareness of what can be achieved after a potentially life changing injury. After thirteen days and over one hundred and seventy nautical miles covered we made our final destination and in doing so managed to enter the record books.

To hear what the town of Ludlow is doing to get behind those in the Armed Forces with 'Ludlow Food Heroes' is truly inspiring and one of the best boosts to morale one can experience whilst on operations. My only regret is that I won't be there over the summer to try some of the delicious recipes and produce - I can assure you that the food out here is not a good substitute!

Captain Guy Disney

18th Apr 2012.

FOB OUELLETTE

Afghanistan.

ACKNOWLEDGMENTS

I would like to recognise and thank the following:

Captain Guy Disney

Templar Medical for their generous sponsorship.

Gary Seymour at The Sun Inn for his support in both the 'Auction of Promises' and fund raising contribution, particularly his contribution from the Beer Festival.

Alan Ramsden of Tiger helicopters for his generous contribution although not a 'Ludlow Food Hero' a hero none the less.

Steve Waddingham of Aston Martin for their generous support and contribution to this project.

Kenneth Swift for his meticulous proof reading.

Michelle Gerrard for her contribution of photographs.

The Ministry of Defence Open Access Library.

Mr Jerry Bentley & Mr Maurice Anslow for their interviews of the butchers and grocers of Ludlow.

Rachel Bonness & Andy Bowden of Orphans Press

The reporters and photographers of the Shropshire Star who supported this campaign for the past 18 months.

Mark Williams of Key Cottage Catering for burning some shoe leather and helping out when I was away on military duties.

All of the 'Ludlow Food Heroes' featured in this publication for their generous donations and lots for the 'Auction of Promises'.

BENTLEY'S WINE MERCHANTS OF LUDLOW

Whilst working in The City in the late 1990s Will and Helen Bentley attended the inaugural wine courses at Berry Bros. & Rudd, vintners to the Royals, in their St James's cellars. What started as a good way for us to pass otherwise dreary Monday evenings in February, became a passion that was eventually to lead to the opening of Bentley's Wine Merchants on Castle Square, only a few feet from the ancient gates of Ludlow Castle.

The great wines of the world not only gave us great personal pleasure, but presented an opportunity to start our own business selling a product we loved and the chance to move away from the crowds of London. We learned the trade through professional exams and a year at a top London merchant. An extended honeymoon took us around the world to the USA, Chile, New Zealand and Australia amongst others. Wherever possible we visited regions and wineries, talked to wine-makers and tasted as much as we could. Many of the discoveries we made in over ten months of "tough" wine travel can now be seen on our Ludlow shelves. Wines you will never see in a supermarket.

It was then time to settle down and get the business started. After a lot of research and driving around the UK, we found Ludlow – a beautiful town with Michelin Starred restaurants, a market, traditional butchers and bakers, delicatessens, local produce and a food culture that was not matched by any local access to a decent bottle of wine. On the same day that we put down our deposit on the Castle Square shop, along with the flat above it, we found out that we were expecting for the first time. It was a big day! Matthew joined the family business only two months after we opened our doors for the first time, one week before the Food Festival in 2005.

Our principle wine philosophy is "best of breed" - wines that offer great value in every region and at every price point. While we do stock the great, traditional names of Bordeaux, Burgundy and the Rhône – they are, after all, considered great for a reason – we are always looking for new ideas, producers and grapes from less fashionable areas: for example Rueda in Spain, the Côtes du Ventoux in the Rhône, Nelson in New Zealand, Lebanon and Sicily. Every year and vintage there is something new and exciting to add to our range, and each year we try to visit at least one new region – although, with the arrival of Matthew and the shop, ten month wine odysseys are a thing of the past until he can join the tasting team.

Given Ludlow's food culture and access to wine-friendly fine produce, we are always thinking about food and wine matching. We're always on hand to offer advice and to give our customers the confidence to try something new with their evening meal without breaking the bank. Our range of food-friendly wines has led to us supplying local restaurants, from bistros to Michelin Stars.

DANIEL JONES
ARTISAN
CHOCOLATIER

After working in the hospitality industry for six years and also attaining a first class honours degree in Culinary Arts Management, I now spend my time developing and creating new and innovative chocolates. I have loved working with chocolate and patisserie since the tender age of five, and over the years have learned to 'play' with unusual flavours and textures to create totally unique designs. I also hold a qualification in sugar, marzipan and chocolate skills, so I can also demonstrate my creativity and artistic skills by creating edible figurines.

I have previously worked as a Sous Chef and Pastry Chef at Hugh Fearnley-Whittingstall's restaurant 'River Cottage', where I started to establish my own cooking style. I then moved to working in Presteigne as Head Chef at The Harp Inn, developing my skills further every day. In every job, I have always striven to demonstrate my passion for chocolate in both sweet and savoury dishes. I have also trained at the University College of Birmingham, and worked at The Ritz in London, Barbadian restaurant Pom Marine, The Atrium UCB of Birmingham and a range of four star hotels and two rosette restaurants.

After this lengthy period of studying, travelling and working, I decided to return to the wonderful Shropshire countryside, near my childhood home. It seemed only right that my business should begin here in this welcoming community, as Ludlow is the most attractive market town I know - as well as a true foodie haven! My business is all about reviving the art of handmade chocolate, and there seemed no better place to demonstrate such a beautiful craft than in Ludlow. Every one of my products is hand-made and packed, with customers able to see me at work making the chocolates at the Ludlow Food Centre, where the Chocolaterie is based.

I use some of the finest cacao in the world - a rare Trinitatio bean from the Dominican Republic - resulting in a completely unique flavour you will never have tasted before. Blended with some amazing and unique ingredients such as the tonka bean, bee pollen and smoked cacao nib, I hope that each chocolate I make is truly exceptional.

The chocolate is fairly traded and organic, and many of my other ingredients are sourced from ethical suppliers, as well as local businesses where possible as it is important to support other producers in the community. Using the best of Shropshire's produce, I can create seasonal specialities, and also work with local businesses such as Sitting in a Tree Crafts who hand make the bespoke wooden egg cups for my Easter Egg Collection. This all goes a long way to creating a completely unique, local handmade product.

To help the revival of the handmade chocolate industry, I demonstrate on stage at markets and events - including the Ludlow Food Festival - to show how simple it can be to make chocolate bars and truffles at home. I also offer a bespoke wedding favour service, and run workshops to try and tempt Shropshire residents into the chocolate making world…!

I do always try to help charities wherever I can between making chocolate batches. I recently raised £170 in support of the Hope House Children's Hospices, where I gave up meat and fish for one month for terminally ill children and their families.

I also support the work of Help for Heroes, helping to raise money for members of the Armed Forces who have been wounded in service. A hero is defined as someone who "is admired for courage or noble qualities" and the men and women of our Armed Forces certainly deserve this title. We must remember our country's men and women who have become sick or injured during service, and it's wonderful to see the work and support that Help for Heroes can offer them when they return to society. The least we can do is show them respect and do our bit to help.

DELI ON THE SQUARE

M ost people who open the door of Deli-on-the-Square suffer an involuntarily reaction. The first breath of air causes most people to exclaim: "Oh what a gorgeous aroma," according to proprietor, Maggie Wright.

The aroma is rarely the same. It depends what's being ordered at the time the customer walks in. It could be anything from fresh coffee beans being ground, to a ripe Camembert being cut open or the smell of smoked garlic.

Whatever the smell it will take most people's minds back to the days when shopkeepers went out of their way to meet a customer's needs; where a shop was a pleasant place to visit; and a place which you almost always left with a smile on your face.

"Since we started trading eight years ago we have tried to put customers first at Deli-on-the-Square.

"Our customers expect knowledgeable staff. They want to know which cheese we recommend for a particular recipe, what's ripe, what will keep for a dinner party three days hence.

They expect to find good local products and they expect us to know chapter and verse about them. We aim to meet their expectations," says Maggie.

Trained in hotel management and catering, Maggie spent much of her working life managing catering in large establishments before becoming a business support adviser for Shropshire Council. In truth shop keeping is probably in her blood because her father, George Cooper spent all his working life working for the family greengrocers W.S. Stephens in Ludlow.

So when the chance came to take over her own deli in the town where she was born and has lived most of her life, she jumped at it.

Deli-on-the-Square was voted best cheese retailer in the central area for three years in succession and won the national title in 2007. Maggie regularly judges at the annual cheese retail awards and at the Great Taste awards.

She and her staff are known as champions of local produce.

"It's been a source of pride to us that several local producers whom we showcased through tastings at the deli have gone on to become major suppliers in their own right. It's important to give the very small producers a lift.

Having them in the shop to talk to customers as they taste the product really does help them a great deal. The most effective advertising you can have is by word of mouth and personal recommendation.

Locally produced goods are all carefully marked up and sign-posted through the shop. They include free-range ham and pies, cakes, biscuits, quail eggs and ranges of jams, chutneys and preserves.

Ludlow's own vineyard chooses to sell its range through the deli, as do all the local breweries.

When occasion demands and there's a gap in the market not being filled, the deli becomes a producer in its own right. So Ludlow now has two mustards of its own. Many of the major restaurants and catering pubs in the area use Shropshire Lad beer mustard for cooking. Indeed the seed mustard features in sausages from some of the town's award-winning butchers while Ludlow Hot mustard is fast making a name for itself as a must-have condiment for connoisseurs of the hot stuff.

Each year the deli supports a charity so when the idea of a book about Ludlow food producers was put forward to support Help for Heroes, Maggie was keen to support it.

"Many of our customers have sons and daughters serving in the forces and we are only too aware that any one of them could be wounded at any time. Help for Heroes gives real help when and where it is needed so we are delighted to support it."

FARMER'S PRODUCE MARKET

F armer's Produce Market in Ludlow's Mill Street and its extensive stall in the Castle Square market has a long history. The fruit and veg business has been run for the last 23 years by Roger and Robin Farmer but it was their parents, Peter and Mary, who got it all rolling 47 years ago. In those days Robin's parents rented a 25-acre small holding in Corvedale from Lord Boyne and they kept poultry, cattle and sheep. Getting just nine pence for a laying hen did not seem good business so in 1963 the Farmers decided to do better and set up shop in Ludlow market. They sold dressed poultry, eggs and a small amount of produce. Mary also made cakes and looked after the selling of herbs and flowers.

Robin remembers well those early days. He was about ten years old and stayed at home on market days to look after the pigs and poultry. He recalls that his parents used to keep his baby brother, Roger, sleeping soundly in

a cardboard box under the market stall. Ludlow market was very different in those days. There was one market on a Monday and Saturday where trading finished at 1pm. There would be four or five little vegetable stalls but the number visiting the market would be double what we see today. Eventually the market also opened on a Friday and the trading day was extended.

Robin attended the old Ludlow Grammar School and went on to Oxford where he studied chemistry. After working for ICI for ten years Robin eventually joined the family business and today he and brother Roger are two of the most familiar faces in the Castle Square market. Mary is still going strong and looks after the flower sales while also doing all the bookwork! The large Mill Street shop started up in 1988 when the old Town Hall was demolished and remains headquarters despite the high profile of the market stall.

"I'm not in it for the money", quips Robin. "But I enjoy what I do and I try to make the people I serve happy", he says. Robin says that business has been affected by parking restrictions and the arrival of the supermarkets. The recent closure of Woolworths has also meant less people coming to Castle Square, he says. But anyone visiting Ludlow on market day sees the Farmer's stall is always popular with that buzz that comes from people enjoying their shopping. About half by value of all their sales represents local produce of which they are great aficionados. Potatoes, asparagus and melons from Bridgnorth, apples from Tenbury, Pembridge and Bromyard, strawberries and raspberries from Ashford Carbonell, green veg and broccoli from Ombersley, runner beans from Worcester. The list is endless. The Farmer's growing nursery plant section is also local with growers coming from Orleton, Bridgnorth and Wolverhampton.

Today, Robin notices that customers buy less of "traditional" vegetables like cabbage, leeks and cauliflower and are more inclined to go for asparagus, spinach, celeriac, fennel, while purple sprouting broccoli is definitely "in". In 47 years Robin says his family business has missed less than six of the scheduled market days. The business is patronised by some of Ludlow's big food names including the Michelin-starred restaurants Underhills and Le Becasse and top establishments like De Greys, Dinham Hall and The Feathers. It's loyalty that counts. One of their the very first customers from all those years ago still comes and always asks for "half a stone of potatoes".

FRANCIS BUTCHERS

Andrew is a master butcher with years of experience, twenty of these in Ludlow. For fifteen years, Andrew had the franchise for the in store butchers in Kwiksave which is now the Coop/Somerfield.

In 2005, he took over the current premises and started the business, as we now know it. He brought with him key colleagues from the Kwiksave days, and so he had the backing to establish the new business rapidly. Now there are seven full time butchers, one part time and two trainees – the latter a welcome and unusual sight these days- as well as a driver.

The shop, with its prominent position, is spacious and user friendly, with a wide range of meats and meat products on display. Traditional names like

Hereford and Welsh Black occur among the prime cuts of local beef, as well as Aberdeen Angus from further afield. Then on through the home made pies, burgers and scotch eggs to the game from local shoots, and so on to Andrew's speciality – venison. There are plenty of deer in local areas such as Mortimer Forest, and in our health-conscious age Andrew has developed this niche market to the point where he is providing up to three hundred deer – mainly roe and fallow – to his ready customers. Lean, tasty and healthy – and even available in venison burger form for barbecue devotees!

The driver, mentioned above, is a reflection of the development of a very significant wholesale business. Andrew is proud of his role in supplying other establishments – for example, the two Michelin-starred restaurants, Mr. Underhill's and La Becasse.

Francis's is also one of only two suppliers contracted to provide meat to Shropshire County Council Schools.

Still, the heart of the business is the shop, cheerful and efficient, and an important part of the community.

GRIFFITHS
BUTCHERS

Master Butcher Alan is the nephew of the owner, Douglas Griffiths. Ludlow born, he stems from a long line of local butchers – his grandfather is still involved in their original business at nearby Leintwardine.

Already well established with a butchers and slaughterhouse at the Leintwardine base, the Griffiths family seized the opportunity to expand into Ludlow when the present shop became available twenty years ago.

The shop had been a butcher's before this – Jones – Mister not Corporal! But it had closed two years before. However, to launch the re-opening, the premises were given what today would be termed 'a complete makeover'. It still combines modernity, with a long, light display counter, with the traditional effect of white and blue background tiling.

Both Griffiths' shops are part of an integrated business, starting at the slaughterhouse.

This supplies the two shops, and also provides a unique service to the other local butchers and the Ludlow Food Centre. It is the easily reached centre for locally raised animals, as well as the hub for a widespread delivery service covering neighbouring counties. The total of staff at the two sites is a substantial eighteen.

The combined experience of the six butchers at Ludlow totals many years, and they are 'all rounders' to a man. Being willing and able to tackle any of the many challenges in butchering is an approach which suits everyone involved.

Over ninety percent of the produce is local, including venison and game, and delicacies such as pigeon, mallard and even cajun chicken! Naturally, the sausages are a matter of pride, and are all produced at Leintwardine. Pies, hot and cold, are cooked on site at Ludlow. And if you want the right sauce, chutney or jelly to bring out the best in your meat, these are prominently displayed in the shop – so it's a one-stop shop for Sunday lunch.

HOBSONS BREWERY

Hobsons Brewery was founded by father and son Jim and Nick Davis with the first brew recorded on Easter Saturday 1993; unfortunately we binned this after 5 hours! The second brew on Easter Sunday worked well after some major rethinks during the Saturday night. Housed in a converted saw mill in Cleobury Mortimer, we sourced second hand equipment, which was adapted to create a 10 barrel plant. One of the original Stainless Fermenters was a lipstick mixing tank in its former life, a lot of the other vessels came from the Carriage Works at Severn Valley Railway where they had mothballed a brewery some years earlier. On the whole this little brewery provided us with reasonable beer, long hours, hot sultry summer days and freezing winter times. The aim was always to prove to ourselves that we could produce a consistently interesting low gravity product, apart from being hobby home brewers none of us had any experience prior to this rash move.

It was thought that as keen ale drinkers there was a need to meet the regional demand for a product that would sit on the bar alongside national brands and others, predominantly Banks's bitter. The original brew 'Hobsons Best Bitter' was well received and production was up to capacity. It was time to seek out larger and more appropriate premises. Those of you, and there are quite a few, who have visited during the past years will see that we currently occupy an old brick built granary on Newhouse Farm. On moving in 1995 we were able to double our production to 70 barrels weekly, also allowing us to double the brewlength.

In late 2001 a red brick second brewery was constructed next to the original. All Best Bitter production is continued at the old brewery, while Town Crier and Old Henry is produced at the state-of-the-art brick one. The national press continued to tell us that sales of Mild nationally were on the floor and that major brewers were pulling these product lines. We took this as an opportunity to develop our own Mild, dark, nutty and 3.2% ABV; this has proved popular in the most unexpected outlets and won the biggest accolade in British brewing – the CAMRA Champion Beer of Britain 2007.

To provide greater national and regional coverage we have installed a bottling plant and commenced packaging of five different bottled beers, these are chill-filtered and reseeded, allowing a controlled secondary fermentation resulting in bottled life of one year.

At Hobsons we have stayed true to our local roots and ethos of running a sustainable business and having fun along the way. We are dedicated to producing our outstanding beers using the finest quality locally sourced ingredients and working closely with producers such as our hop grower Geoff Thompson some seven miles down the road. We have set up a group of growers in the South Shropshire area to plant one of the oldest and premium varieties of malting barley, Maris Otter. Sourcing the very best ingredients combined with the craftsmanship of our brewers has set the flavour of Hobsons apart and gained recognition in the form of awards like the CAMRA Champion Beer of Britain 2007 and CAMRA regional beer of the year 2011, to name but two.

Our commitment to supporting local communities does not end with the sourcing of ingredients; we are passionate about promoting local pubs, businesses and community spirit as a whole. You will often find Hobsons championing our publicans, supporting local sports teams, getting involved in events, we even have our own troop of Sea Shanty singers!

In 2011 we worked on a special project with our local Royal British Legion branch, brewing a beer to commemorate their 90th anniversary. The beer "Old Comrade" allowed us not only to donate a percentage of sales to the Poppy Appeal (over £1300) but to get involved in local events and celebrations in our home town of Cleobury Mortimer.

Sticking to traditional brewing methods doesn't mean we turn away from new thinking. We make best use of all emerging green technologies and harness the environmental assets where we live. We embarked on a project that we hoped would help us achieve our aim to be the country's leading sustainable brewery, by utilising technologies such as a ground source heat pump system, rainwater harvesting system and lightweight packaging. To enhance the efficiency of the ground source heat pump in 2007 we installed an 11kw GAIA Wind turbine, a pretty twin blade design that powers about a third of the brewery's requirements.

Whatever we do, we will always strive for best practice in our brewing and bottling processes and we will continue to be innovative in the ways we support our environment and community.

KEY COTTAGE CATERING

Well I suppose it all started many years before it came to fruition. I had been sitting in an office for more years than I care to remember, earning a not inconsiderable salary and although totally dedicated to my job and enjoying the benefits it brought, I was really a person who wanted to "have a go" at his own business and stand or fall on my ability's before it was too late.

I had always had an interest in cooking, mainly fostered by having to cook for both myself and my mother soon after my father passed away at an early age. As time passed, teenage years, marriage & children, my love of cooking remained. One day a neighbour asked if I would cater for a small gathering, so I did, which then started, I suppose, a bit of a hobby. I started

to cater for the occasional event: birthdays, dinner parties etc. So I suppose it was inevitable that at some juncture I would follow a path into outside catering and home-produced foods.

I started the business by making a number of different free range pork sausages like Pork and Ludlow Gold, Pork and oven-roasted pepper, and even a Beef & Guinness sausage for the Boot pub in Orleton. These I sold in and around the pubs and restaurants and was enjoying it greatly.

However I soon realised that although this was great fun, it was hardly going to pay the bills, I had to move on. I decided to try my hand at selling in Ludlow market.

With this in mind I was really at a loss as to exactly what I might sell on the market stall. I therefore decided to make a load of sausages and having just taught myself to cold smoke, produced a kiln-full of salmon. So armed to the teeth with sausages and salmon it was off to market to sell and talk to people to try and find out what they would like to see being sold. This lesson was invaluable. I came back with more ideas than you could shake a stick at, some totally unworkable and some inspired.

After a short period I devised a recipe for my own make of Pork Pies. This I was told would be a good seller especially if I made them from local free range meat. So pork pies really were the first volume selling product I made. With a meat to fat ratio of 80 / 20, which is far higher than a commercially made pie, using herbs from the garden and a good pastry, I was onto a winner.

As the pork pies were selling so well I had a chat with our local shoot captain and enquired what they did with the game they had harvested during the season? I was told they didn't have a lot spare once guns, beaters and local land owners had a brace or two but I was welcome to the rest, for a price of course. Armed with a few pheasants and a more than a few ideas the next pie to come onto the menu was Pheasant & Port-soaked sultana.

These flew off the shelves (excuse the pun) and we now make a much larger range of game pies, for example Venison and Cassis and Wild Duck and Apricot.

Seasonality is important to me. Once the game season is finished, the game pies are finished. I now make a range of Chicken pies to tide me over until the game season starts again and as I write, I am making Chicken & Asparagus but that will be off the menu next month because the asparagus season is drawing to an end, so we will substitute possibly a chicken and home smoked gammon, anyway you get the idea.

From my home smoked salmon and hand made pies right the way through to our wild Cray fish sandwiches, ALL the produce we make is totally additive and preservative free. True it reduces the longevity of the product, but who wants to eat bread that has a shelf life of two weeks or a crab pate that lasts for a month?

Good food, seasonally produced and locally grown is our maxim. Not always possible, but always tried for.

So thanks to old customers and new and I look forward to boring the pants off you when you come and ask me "how do you produce that"...

LUDLOW BREWERY

Ludlow has a strong reputation for real ale but the town had been without its own brewery since the 1930s when closure came to the Ludlow and Craven Arms Brewery. That was until May 2006 when Gary and Alison Walters opened the Ludlow Brewing Company in an old outbuilding of a haulier's yard at the bottom of Corve Street.

Gary was a carpenter by trade but he had long held a fascination with brewing and he was a frequent visitor to real ale festivals. He started experimenting with brewing at home and he was always led by what he liked most in a real ale. So when Gary and his wife started up their brewery in Ludlow the first ale was a "gold", which within months had won best ale at the CAMRA Severn Valley Railway beer festival. Ludlow Gold was soon followed by three other quality ales. First came the lovely malty "Boiling Well" which is named after a nearby spot on the River Corve where the water always seems to "boil" just before the river starts to rise. This was followed by a copper-coloured "Best" and a ruby-black stout with a sweet, nutty flavour called "Black Knight".

By 2008 it was clear that the brewery was running out of space and so when an abandoned Victorian railway shed on the same site became available it was time to make a major commitment. Gary and Alison brought together a half a million pound investment which included help from Advantage West Midlands and Shropshire Tourism. The conversion was opened in 2011 and the building now houses a brand new 20 barrel brewing system complete with a Brewery Tap and Visitor Centre which can also be used as an events venue. The brewery has three fermenters and the extra capacity has allowed the introduction of a fifth ale. This is called "Stairway", an extra pale ale which has proved to be an instant success. Stairway, unusually, uses a lager hop known as Sladek. Gary usually uses hops grown locally at Little Lambswick, Lindridge, and his barley is the very traditionally British variety Maris Otter.

Gary is a great believer in small breweries and he has no real desire to expand much further. He does not like notching up "beer miles" and does not want to sell outside a 40-mile radius. Today the new brewery is producing at the rate of 50 barrels a week and it has around 60 pubs as regular customers.

Gary wants to work locally supplying sports clubs and he already numbers Ludlow's cricket, rugby, football and golf clubs amongst his customers.

Gary is proud of his business's green credentials and the environmentally friendly brewery has developed a unique system of cooling. The brewery uses a dry air source heat pump which extracts any warmth from the cooling process to provide the building's own heat. The pump can extract warmth from the air even on a cool day and from every kilowatt of cooling 3.5 kilowatts of heating is produced.

Gary is happy to support Help for Heroes. He says with feeling," I get very moved when I see the parades through Wootton Bassett – it does bring it home."

Ludlow Castle
& Festival

Ludlow has been described as one of the most beautiful towns in the UK. It's also the home of one of the best-loved food festivals in the UK. The Ludlow Food Festival organisers hold three events each year; the Spring Festival held the second weekend of May; the Magnalonga, a seven mile walk with local food and drink at strategic stops on route; and the jewel in the crown, The Ludlow Food Festival held the second weekend in September. With its fabulous mix of passionate local producers, top class workshops and events that stretch way beyond the festival's venue within the historic castle walls, it's easy to see why The Ludlow Food Festival continues to attract both residents and visitors from far and wide.

It's hard to imagine now, but the Ludlow Food Festival started after a conversation around a kitchen table when local foodies and traders were looking for a way of preserving the town centre and its eclectic range of shops.

The main idea was to create a festival which would both promote the area's small food and drink producers and encourage visitors to explore Ludlow's fascinating shops, restaurants and pubs. In 1995 this was a novel idea which, it was freely admitted, was done "just to see what happened". The venue was not a problem - the castle square with its traditional open-air market and the town's historic castle (used from the second year onwards) provided the perfect backdrop.

The festival was an immediate success thanks to the response from those same food and drink producers and suppliers - and the band of volunteer helpers who gathered to stage the event. They had no instruction book; nothing like it had ever been tried before. But they were enthusiastic, committed and imaginative - and willing to work hard.

Equally importantly, they decided from the start that the event had to be fun as well, both for them and for those taking part, despite the underlying serious objective of promoting the businesses of the Marches and the area itself.

In 2000 the event saw visitor numbers reach more than 12,000 paying customers visiting the tented village in the castle. Since then the festival has grown, with the peak being achieved in 2010 with over 21,000 food lovers enjoying the event.

Whether you visit the Spring Festival or the main Food Festival in September, there's plenty to see and do.

Spring highlights include the 140 plus beers brought to Ludlow with the help of SIBA, the Society of Independent Brewers. No matter what your real ale tastes, you are bound to find a pint that satisfies. You'll also find more than 60 local producers, a whole host of beer and food writers, chefs and culinary experts ready to share their passion for everything food and drink.

Car enthusiasts will also appreciate The Marches Transport Festival, which forms part of the Spring Festival. Get up close and personal with gorgeous classics from the pre-war era to the 1980's.

September is all about food, food, food (and drink)! Around 160 of the finest artisan producers and small independent food and drink businesses exhibited at Ludlow in 2011. From the finest cheeses to the tastiest breads, mouth watering cakes to hand reared meats, every single exhibitor is hand picked by the organisers to ensure only the best products are on offer.

Ludlow Food Festival really is the place to see experts in their field show off their culinary skills; as well as local chefs, Chris Bradley and Will Holland, a whole host of the best chefs in the UK love to visit the festival and take part in what's been termed Michelin Friday.

Just sit back, relax and listen to the masters of food divulge their tricks of the trade or join in with interactive sessions such as bread making and knife skills.

For food connoisseurs the Slow Food Taste Workshops are a must. Led by expert producers or chefs they will guide you through specific products or genres with a unique tutored tasting.

The competitions have always been a really popular part of the festival with talented and passionate members of the public, as well as professionals, submitting their finest creations for scrutiny. In 2011 the way the competitions were judged was changed to make them an event in their own right.

The competitions now take place in late August with a panel of judges sampling all manner of delectable dishes. Categories include bread, cakes, pork pies, sandwiches, strawberry jam, non- alcoholic fruit cordial and the top award 'Best New Product'.

For a less formal, but no less tasty experience, try one of the festival trails. The Ludlow Food Festival has always extended beyond the confines of the castle. One of the most popular aspects of the September festival are the trails, including the sausage, ale and bread trails around town which sell out early over the weekend. Over all 3 days there's also the window dressing competition throughout the town with more than 40 shops taking part.

Finally, it's not strictly a trail, but if you have a sweet tooth - pudding tasting at the Methodist Church is a must.

As a not-for-profit organisation, the team behind the Food Festival is always looking for ways to give back to producers and the community. A few years ago a bursary was set up to help young people start their careers in the food and drink industry and last year an exhibitor bursary was also introduced to allow new or smaller producers, who are unable to produce enough to attend the festival all three days, to be part of the festival.

In addition the festival also raises money for local and international charities including Self Help Africa and the Mayor's charity, such as The Ludlow Foyer. One of more than 130 organisations in the UK accredited by the Foyer Federation, it is dedicated to providing a supportive environment for young people moving towards independence.

Skillbuilders is a Ludlow based volunteer project dedicated to enhancing the skills of the next generation. A strong supporter of the educational element of the food festival, the team will welcome dozens of local school children to Ludlow during the festival for dedicated demonstrations with a number of professional chefs and colleges.

In addition, Friday afternoon sees the Young Chef Contest take place. It celebrates the achievements of young chefs in Ludlow and the Marches and the skilled chefs who mentor and tutor them.

We have had the army exhibiting with us for many years, showing people how they cook on the Soyer stove and selling scrumptious stew to raise money for charity. It is an important link for the festival and an area that is much enjoyed by the public as it's both informative and delicious!

The Ludlow Food Festival is proud to be supporting Help For Hero's. Beth Heath, Operations Director added: "The work undertaken by Help For Hero's is truly inspirational. Their aim is purely to help and support ordinary people doing extraordinary things and that is a goal we can identify with."

LUDLOW FOOD CENTRE

Ludlow Food Centre was opened in April 2007 to give food lovers the opportunity to buy the region's best produce. The Centre sources more than 80% of its produce from Shropshire and neighbouring counties of Worcestershire, Herefordshire and Powys. It employs over 80 local people, many of which work in the 8 production kitchens that surround the retail shop. These kitchens make half the food sold in the Centre and include a jam and pickle kitchen, butchery, bakery, production kitchen, dairy, coffee roasting room and a packaging room. All the kitchens have windows that face in to the retail area so that customers can watch their food being made as they shop. The Centre's philosophy is to sell fresh, local, seasonal and handmade food that is of the highest quality and over the years it has picked up a number of national and international awards.

Positioned to the north of Ludlow on the A49, the Food Centre is part of the Earl of Plymouth's Oakly Park Estate. The Estate provides all the beef, lamb and rare breed Gloucester Old Spot pork for the Centre's butchery along with a selection of seasonal vegetables from Lady Windsor's walled garden. Ludlow is renowned as a foodie mecca and the Food Centre has certainly added to its appeal. The Food Centre is essentially a microcosm of the traditional British high street but also acts as a hub for local producers

to sell their abundant produce throughout the year. In the summer local farmers and growers supply fresh fruit such as strawberries, raspberries, plums and tomatoes. In the winter there are root vegetables and brassicas such as parsnips, carrots and sprouts. Throughout the year the Centre makes a wide variety of seasonal specialities including deli food, pies, ready meals, cheeses, jams, pickles, breads and cakes that utilise the abundant seasonal produce from the area.

We are always looking for ways to contribute to Ludlow's heritage, its reputation and its people. We have been involved in the Ludlow Food Festival since we opened and we work with organisations, businesses and producers in the town who make and support great food. We are proud of our region, the people who work for us, and we have the utmost respect for our customers because they understand what real food is all about. Our Estate has a long history and involvement in the area, and today it is home to hundreds of local people including many of our workers. Ludlow is important to us because it defines who we are, what we do and why we do it. We are committed to highlighting the quality of the produce from our fields, the skills of our producers, and to upholding Ludlow's reputation as the best place to buy and eat food outside of London.

By featuring in this publication we want to demonstrate what Ludlow and the Food Centre stands for, why this area is renowned for its food and why we all believe in supporting Help for Heroes. The efforts made by our forces can only be admired. We are all humbled by the commitment and sacrifices they have made to keep us safe and improve the lives of others. If our serving men and women are willing to give and risk so much, then we believe they should be supported, whether in the field or at home, and we are proud to have contributed to this publication.

LUDLOW STOVES

L udlow Stoves was born out of necessity. When looking to buy a boiler for our 400 year old, half timbered cottage, we simply couldn't afford oil or gas. The range cookers which we loved the look of were very expensive too. After a holiday to Italy we noticed that everyone cooked and heated their homes by wood. After some investigation we imported one directly from the manufacturer and were delighted with our choice which heats all of our house, we have ample hot water, large hot plate and oven. Everyone commented how warm our house was and how lovely it looked and where could they get theirs from. Having been together for over 20 years Gregg and Corrabeth wanted to work together and this seemed to be the ideal opportunity. Gregg runs a building and renovation company, Creative Property Developments which specialises in older buildings. He fits kitchens, bathrooms, brick and block and everything in between. He has trained as a Hetas qualified engineer to install the stoves too. Each business complements the other, the only problem is, when a client finds out what he can do they hand him a list of jobs!

We sell over 90 different types of stoves, cookers and pellet heaters so we usually have something for everyone. Turning to wood as a heat source is a lifestyle choice and people need the full information before purchasing a stove. Our customers find coming to the Showroom and seeing a stove and a range cooker working in a family home reassuring. As our children are young, having a showroom at home was the ideal answer, we can open during the day and also evenings and weekends too, which gives clients a more flexible time to come and visit.

We source many cookers and stoves from Italy because they are beautifully crafted, have excellent efficiency and are far less expensive than other stoves and cookers on the market. The Italians are renowned for design and style and the companies we deal with are family businesses that have been manufacturing for over 50 years and are very quick to respond to bespoke finishes that our customers require.

When choosing a wood burning cooker there are many considerations that need to be taken into account before making a purchase. Cooking and heating on wood is a lifestyle choice which may mean you need to take a slower pace. Modern technology means that the old fashioned ranges which were temperamental, hard to keep lit and cooked with different hot spots are a thing of the past. A secondary burn on many models make the efficiency very high and economical, alongside being carbon neutral.

When choosing a stove you need to take into account how large your room is, whether you want to heat the whole house from a boiler version, or simply watch the flames in a cosy armchair. Pellet heaters offer a very convenient option where small wooden pellets are fed from a hopper giving a small flame which are totally automatic and can be timed according to your needs.

We have travelled a lot over the years however Ludlow and Shropshire are where our hearts belong. We feel very privileged to have such a beautiful, unspoilt area to live in and we wanted to bring up our children, as we had, messing around in streams, camping and generally getting into mischief.

The Ludlow food festival highlights the fantastic local food that is available and home cooking is such an important part to many families lives. Having a wood burning oven only enhances this as it is a real focal point to any kitchen and always attracts friends eager to warm their bums!

Being able to support Help for Heroes is very important to me. I think having children only enhances my feelings. Explaining to them how other people are not as fortunate as us and that there are men and women who bravely fight and die for our liberty is very humbling. Supporting the cause and promoting their awareness is imperative.

LUDLOW VINEYARD & DISTILLERY

L udlow Vineyard & Distillery is a family business run by Mike and Barbara Hardingham from their farmhouse in Clee St Margaret, about 5 miles from Ludlow on the Brown Clee. Their holding includes a 10-acre vineyard, a cider orchard, a winery, a cider-barn, a bottling facility, a distillery and, somewhat bizarrely, 200 walnut trees which they planted in 1999. The operation produces wine, cider, apple juice, spirits, liqueurs and pickled walnuts.

This venture is an early retirement activity for Mike and Barbara. Barbara worked for the UK Atomic Energy Authority in Oxfordshire as a Financial Administrator, while Mike worked in I.T. in Oxfordshire, and Banking (in London). Neither of these career paths seem to lead directly to food and drink production, so how did they end up in Ludlow making alcohol?

It all started when Mike and Barbara first met in Oxfordshire nearly 30 years ago, and set up home in a small village near a vineyard. Mike caught the bug! He used to go along at weekends to help at the vineyard, then he joined the industry associations, read lots of books, and persuaded Barbara that it was a good idea. After many man-days of planting, and many man-months of pruning, Barbara is now not quite so sure how she got talked into it!

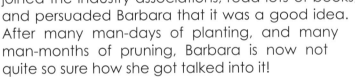

But why plant a vineyard near Ludlow? It turns out that Barbara was born and raised at Hayton's Bent, and went to the Girls High School in Ludlow, so Mike and Barbara used to come here regularly, and Mike fell in love with the place. So when some land and a house came up for sale in Clee St Margaret, they jumped at the chance and they started planting vines in 1995. They moved permanently to Clee St Margaret in 2001, but Mike continued to work part time in London, catching the train in Birmingham several times a week. In 2007 Mike gave up banking for good and started doing the drinks business full time.

At Clee St Margaret's altitude, the grape harvest is rarely good enough to keep the enterprise busy, so with all the wine making equipment being under-used, diversification into Cider and Apple Juice soon followed. Meanwhile, in the long dark winter evenings, Mike was working on his long term goal, the holy grail of alcohol production: to get a licence for a distillery! It wasn't easy and it took a long time to get through all the hoops, but eventually the Excise people were happy and at the end of 2009 a gleaming pile of copper and stainless steel arrived from Germany. The distillery, or "Mike's Latest Toy" as it is referred to by Barbara, is now producing apple brandy and other spirits such as Pear and Apple Eau de Vie, and various sweet liqueurs. There is also some grape brandy on its way, and Mike's latest experiment is the Shropshire Prune Damson Eau de Vie, inspired by the success of the Ludlow Marches Slow Food branch in getting the Shropshire Prune listed in the "Ark of Taste".

While Mike plays with the alcoholic toys, Barbara is responsible for the accounting and the budgets, and she watches the pounds no less carefully than when she was dealing with the European Commission's millions for the Atomic Energy programme. Thanks to her prudent stewardship of the finances, the enterprise is now making them enough to live on. "The Distillery is Mike's last expensive toy" she jokes, with a good-natured but deadly serious glint in her eye. "Sad, but true" agrees Mike.

PRICE'S BAKERS

S.C Price & Sons is owned by Sheila Barnett, her daughters, Wendy and Deborah, and Deborah's husband, Peter.

The business has been run in Ludlow by the family since 1940, when it was bought from Mr Davies & Mr Brown, by Sidney Price. He ran the bakery and shops with his wife, with the help of several of his 12 children! All this while finding time to serve three terms as Ludlow's mayor.

Sid passed away in 1977 and the business passed on to his sons, Gerald and Trevor, and daughter, Sheila. All this time, the bread was baked in a traditional brick oven at the bake house, across the other side of Castle Square, in Quality Square. As the ovens were unloaded, eager customers would look out for the bread being brought across the square to the shop. Deliveries were made around the town and surrounding countryside by horse & cart, then later by a fleet of vans.

In 1990, Deborah and Peter moved back to Ludlow from successful management careers in London restaurants. After setting up the take-away

sandwich and filled rolls section of the shop, Peter began work in the bakery to learn from the older hands, and Deborah shared the running of the shop with her mother.

In 2004, Wendy also became a partner in the business. We have also moved our bakery to a custom-built building directly behind the shop, in the old garden, with modern fuel-efficient electric ovens. And so our 68 year presence on Ludlow's Castle Square continues, with generations of the town's families enjoying the pleasure of a Price's loaf .

We have been providing a personal, individual and friendly service to generations of Ludlow's residents and many visitors.

We bake on our premises six days a week, using modern ovens in a purpose-built bakehouse at the rear of the shop.

Price's have always made our bread with traditional fermentation methods where the most important ingredient is time. Good bread can't be rushed!

Apart from our standard range of breads and pastries, we are always happy to bake to order - we haven't been defeated by a special request yet!

We are always keen to help charities with local links and we think that nearly every family has some connection with members of the armed services. That is why we are proud to support Help For Heroes.

PRICE'S FISHMONGER

I have been trading successfully on The Ludlow Market site for the past 31 years for 3-4 days per week. I employ local staff, two who have worked for me for over 25 years, and are very keen and helpful for customers' needs.

I buy fresh top quality from fish ports around the British Isles. I also buy game from local farms and shoots in Shropshire. Quality food products have always been my priority for our customers. I sell a variety of fresh fish when in season, as many as 30 plus different species regularly. I also supply local hotels and restaurants in the area.

Ludlow is fortunate to be able to offer a wonderful choice of individual shops and also has a market in the middle of the town four days a week.

It is known as a gourmet town for food, with good restaurants and hotels and its food festival every year in September. These attract shoppers and tourists from surrounding counties, i.e. Worcestershire, Herefordshire and the West Midlands, who like the individual and personal service a small business can provide.

I support the Help for Heroes for its commitment to help the injured who have served in the armed forces for our country.

PURE SPIRITS

Described as a 'sweet shop for adults', Pure Spirit Drinks is a family run specialist drinks retailer based in Old Street, Ludlow. The business is one of only a few specialist whisky shops in England – selling whiskies from around the globe as well as a fine selection of Scottish malts from hard-to-find distilleries and smaller producers. Much more than a 'traditional whisky shop', Pure Spirit Drinks also lists over 300 bottled beers, local cider / perry and an extensive range of fine spirits and wines. The business also ships internationally and has one of the UK's most extensive drinks websites.

If you fancy knowing more about malt whiskies, or just looking to widen your horizons, the shop's proprietor, Stephen Hay, offers small group and 1-2-1 expert tastings. A great place to while away half an hour or so on a rainy afternoon in Ludlow. With a dram in hand, Stephen explains:

'We wanted to create a destination for purchasing some of the world's greatest drinks, from fine whiskies, exceptional brandies through to the very best of local products. To this end we often source direct from suppliers, allowing us to source unusual and often unique items, including single cask whiskies and limited edition beers. Part of our shopping experience is about allowing customers to sample and explore items as they arrive in stock, to make the shopping experience more intimate, lively and informative. I was once told that whisky selling is a personal business, and I very much support this philosophy. Over 80% of our physical shop stock is sold by hand, which allows customers to discuss and explore the quality of the products'.

With a passion for whiskies, Stephen can also provide expert advice on investing in whiskies, selling rare malts and even the best bars and distilleries to visit, should you wish to take your interest further!

Pure Spirit Drinks chose to open their shop in Ludlow to build upon the town's reputation for independent retailers and food-focused businesses. Stephen explains:

'For several years we have been looking to open a retail outlet in Ludlow, attracted by the town's markets, Slow Food status and the rich mix of independent shops. The town offers quite a distinctive shopping alternative to bland shopping centres and multiple-dominated High Streets. From our previous shop in South Staffordshire, we had also traded with a wide range of Shropshire businesses, including brewers and cider makers and therefore Ludlow felt like a natural home for us to grow our businesses'.

Both members of the Heart of England Fine Foods (HEFF) and Shropshire Tourism, Pure Spirit Drinks is a strong supporter of local producers, retailing a substantial range of local products from across Shropshire, Herefordshire and Gloucestershire. During the summer months you can also sample and take-home local cider and perry, which can be found on draught in the Ludlow shop.

Stephen adds: 'Whenever possible we try and get out and about to meet suppliers to get a feel for their business and products; it all helps us to help customers make better decisions, when choosing local beers, ciders and spirits. We are also looking forward to developing our approach to working with local businesses on pairing premium drinks with local produce. In the past, we have worked with Appleby's on matching fine cheeses with single malt whiskies – a great alternative to traditional wine and cheese events'.

Stephen adds:

'We are extremely pleased to be supporting Help for Heroes; it is a national charity we have supported in the past through auctioning rare drinks, and appreciate the very direct practical support it provides the men and women of our armed forces. The charity is also clearly focusing upon long-term lasting benefits rather than just short-term projects, which deliver lasting support to injured members of our armed forces as they move on to the next stage of their lives, often overcoming very difficult physical and emotional injuries'.

RICKARDS

There is no doubt that Ludlow is a town well blessed with historic buildings and we are proud that at our premises in the Bull Ring we have managed to protect our unique heritage whilst remaining a vibrant and successful business.

There have been ironmongers trading on this site since the late eighteenth century with Heber Rickards, the founder of our company, taking up residence at No.7 in around 1864. Within a few years he had acquired No.6 and expanded the business.

Remarkably little has changed since that time; the original shop fittings and drawers are still in daily use, as are the upstairs rooms which were the family's home until about 1901. Those rooms boast many interesting features including period William Morris wallpaper and a lovely 19th C ceiling rose. The 'Managing Directors Office' looks out onto the courtyard through a superb curved window and retains its original panelling and cupboards.

In what was the family's kitchen, the evocative old stone flags provide a characterful background to our displays and the unusual tank which fed water to the sink is still in evidence.

The most ancient part of the building forms the rear of the courtyard; it seems to be of an earlier date than the front sections and includes what was a stable. The old storage bins for loose nails are here, as is a fascinating collection of old paraffin lamps and heaters, some of which still have their stock tickets attached, and amongst which are two 'Garage Stoves', popular for keeping Rolls Royces warm during cold Edwardian winters.

But Rickards is far more than an interesting collection of old buildings or a quaint survival of an earlier age. It is part of the fabric of the town and of the local community and is held in great affection both by those who shop with us and the staff, past and present, who have worked for us.

There is a great tradition of long service with the company, personified by our oldest member of staff, Harold Edwards. Although retired, Harold, we are pleased to say, still works one day a week, and we greatly value his extensive experience, as do the many customers who ask for him personally.

Sybil Marsh, who retired as manager three years ago after forty years with the firm, still maintains a regular involvement and has many memories of her working life at Rickards; much of it alongside another long serving employee, Gill Ingram, who notched up more than thirty years' service.

We hold regular cooking demonstrations throughout the year in the Old Kitchen, one of the most popular being the open day which we arrange to coincide with the Food Festival, and it has always been our policy to give as much support as we can both to local charities and events.

Our ranges are evolving to cater to the current market and we regularly supply local chefs with a wide variety of equipment. So, although the shop may be old, the business is as contemporary in its outlook and it's ranging as any of its competitors, and we intend to continue as a Ludlow institution for at least another hundred and forty years.

During its long history, Rickards has waved several members of its staff off to war or into the services.

Some of these earlier employees have left mementoes of their time with the company in the form of graffiti in words and pictures on the walls of the top floor of the building. Judging by the extravagantly moustachioed faces depicted here, some of these gentlemen might possibly have witnessed the end of the Edwardian age on the fields of Flanders. A more recent employee noted on a nearby wall the date that he started at Rickards and the date on which he left to do his national service with the R.A.F. in the late 1940's.

Undoubtedly, employers such as Rickards would have done all they could in the past to help and support staff returning from the services.

Now we all have a responsibility, and an opportunity, to give that help and support to those who have served in modern conflicts, and we at Rickards are proud to be associated with Help for Heroes.

The Church and Charlton Arms

Ludlow's Church Inn has the genuine feel of being the town's headquarters and for real ale fans it is most definitely home. This snug medieval inn always has no less than eight real ales on tap and thanks to owner Graham Willson-Lloyd (locally known as "Floyd") and full time cellarman Mike Sargent they are never less than in perfect condition.

Floyd has championed real ale in Ludlow like no one else and he was jointly responsible with David Gurr-Gearing for re-instating the town's old ale trail which now attracts over 1,000 participants at the time of the Ludlow Food & Drink Festival. Today Floyd is proud of the fact that every one of Ludlow's 16 pubs serves at least one real ale.

The Church Inn has featured guest ales from all over the country but Floyd likes to source locally as much as he can and he has given a showcase to twelve of Shropshire's sixteen breweries. The excellent ales of the Ludlow Brewery - Boiling Well, Ludlow Gold and Black Knight - are always on tap at the Church Inn and Cleobury Mortimer brewer, Hobsons, is also permanently represented. The regular "Session Ale" is Wye Valley Bitter.

Floyd has always been in the vanguard of Ludlow's push to build a reputation as a "slow town" with a flair for good food and drink. Originally from South Wales, he had attended Ludlow's old grammar school and chose the town when he decided he wanted to be an innkeeper. He bought the Church Inn as a free inn in 1999 and immediately began to be a champion for the small food and drink producers that populate the Marches area. The Inn itself became known for its excellent pub grub with its own burgers specially made by local butchers Andrew Francis, a selection of Ludlow's famous sausages, and a reputation for pies that has led to the setting up of Floyd's own "Ludlow Pie Company". At Food Festival time the Church Inn also finds itself a stop-off on the "sandwich", "cake", "pâté", "pudding" as well as, naturally, the "real ale" trails.

Three years after buying the Church Inn, Floyd took over the lease of the wine bar Ego in Quality Square. Ego has a broad menu and it is a perfect choice for a "pre-theatre" when the Shakespeare is on during the summer

at Ludlow Castle. Floyd followed up Ego by acquiring the neighbouring small shop which he converted into "Dali" and which he calls the "quintessential English tea shop" (even though it has a drinks licence!).

Floyd now had a lot on his hands but he still found time to serve on Ludlow's Chamber of Trade & Commerce, where he and many others, including Phil Maile, became the founders of the town's famous Food and Drink Festival. For one year Floyd also served as the town's mayor.

Still bigger challenges, however, lay ahead. Floyd now set his sights on restoring the historic Charlton Arms pub which was slowly sliding into the river Teme down by Ludford Bridge. Dating back to the 18th century, the Charlton was in such disrepair that it had been closed down under Health & Safety regulations in 2004.

Floyd purchased the Charlton in January 2005 and got permission to open it with a temporary bar, some patched-up electrics and a mobile catering van in the car park for food in the summer.

Floyd found that the Charlton was in a dreadful state and it would take many thousands of pounds (including £1,000 for a bat survey!) to restore the place. It was almost a complete rebuild with new floors and doors and a tasteful new extension. The result is stunning and the Charlton now boasts 10 en-suite rooms, a 120-person function suite and a restaurant overlooking the river. The sensitive refurbishment of the Charlton has won Floyd two Heritage Awards. But, true to form, the Charlton serves four real ales and they are also looked after by trusty cellarman Mike.

Today Floyd employs about fifty staff in Ludlow and has every claim to be one of the town's "food heroes". But he has plenty of reason to sympathise with the heroes of our Armed Forces. Floyd's family was very much Army with his father serving in the South Wales Borderers and managing a daring escape from an Italian PoW camp during the Second World War. His father's younger brother Mike is a retired colonel and both his mother's brothers were killed in action during the War. "So I have a certain passion for what our young men are doing these days in the name of peace and democracy," says Floyd.

THE FISH HOUSE

The Fish House is owned by Louise and Andy Hackney. Louise's family have been fishmongers since 1946 and she is the third generation of fishmongers, with the 4th well established with her niece and nephew carrying on the family tradition.

Louise's grandmother Anne Willis started it all when she stood with a barrow on the High Street, Bilston, West Midlands. In those days the fish used to be delivered by train to her from Birmingham Wholesale Market into Bilston train station, where she then used to barrow it into the High Street in all weathers: in winter she said she used to be frozen to the spot it was so cold. The family business is still going strong, with Louise's sister and brother-in-law running MRJ Willis Fish Wholesale in Wolverhampton. This is where Louise sources the fish for The Fish House, ensuring the best quality is provided to you through their long family history. Louise's Grandmother is still fit and well, she will be 100 years old in November 2011 and she's so pleased that the family tradition is continuing in Ludlow.

Louise and Andy came to Ludlow in October 2008, and on visiting the town during their first few weeks they were surprised that there was no Fishmonger established in the town centre. It seemed a big gap in the foodie town renowned for its wonderful butchers, bakers, pubs and restaurants. It took a while for the right location in the town to become available but they didn't lose hope, and when Tolsey House became available in June 2010 they knew it was the place to set-up The Fish House. "It just seemed so natural to create a fishmonger with a bit of a twist, which is where the idea of the taster menu came about. Customers can now try anything from oysters to our seafood platter whilst watching the world go by with a glass of wine. We thought that Ludlow of all places would appreciate something different with the focus on high quality".

Their team at the shop is small but highly skilled and enthusiastic about what they do. Louise's husband Andy is a fitness professional with his own personal training business on the Eco Park in Ludlow but he becomes the 'Saturday Boy' at The Fish House every weekend waiting tables and ensuring their customers are looked after. Tony is a butcher of many years experience now turned fishmonger, and uses his exceptional knife skills at The Fish House.

"Being part of Ludlow Food Heroes for Help 4 Heroes is a great honour. We have been given a fantastic and very special fundraising opportunity being part of this project. The book is something that we can keep for generations to come, not only to celebrate all that is good about the wonderful market town of Ludlow but how we played a part in raising essential funds for a truly worthy charity. Our Servicemen and women are ordinary people just like me but unlike me they are doing extraordinary things in the course of their working day".

THE FRUIT BASKET

The Fruit Basket has been a fixture for the last twenty years in Ludlow's narrow Church Street. All visitors to the town can't help stopping to admire Rob Morris' attractive displays of fruit and veg, but can they imagine the hard work that goes into maintaining such a show of fresh produce? Rob's day starts at 3am when he sets off in his van to buy at Birmingham's Pershore Street central fruit and veg market. Back in Ludlow for 8.30am to set up, and then a long day until closing up at 5.30. Even then Rob will spend much of his evening sorting out produce at his home near Tenbury Wells. Fortunately, help is at hand. Rob's wife Diane, daughter Cara and two of his three sons, Aaron and Ross, help Dad out and Caroline Holmes, who used to be a Ludlow butcher, also works in the shop.

Rob says that the hard work is worth it because he enjoys his customers and gets satisfaction from delivering quality food. Things have changed though over the twenty years Rob has been running the business. When he started, Ludlow had around six fruit and veg shops and business was brisk. The arrival of supermarkets has changed the way people shop, but

fortunately Rob's commitment to good produce and service has earned him the respect of an increasingly discerning clientele. Today's shoppers are better informed about food and there is more demand for things like sweet potatoes, butternut squash, fennel and coriander. Rob notices that customers are particularly fussy about potatoes of which there are now a bewildering number of varieties. Rob explains that "Maris Piper" potatoes are the best for chips and roasting, "Wilja" for boiling and "Estima" is the best all-rounder. But then it all depends on the season. You are likely to see Egyptian or Majorcan potatoes on Rob's display during early spring, which then give way to Cornish and Pembrokes in April/May and various local varieties from June onwards.

In true Ludlow tradition Rob is a devotee of local produce. During the course of the year The Fruit Basket sources around 50% of its produce from up to thirty local suppliers. Whether it's carrots from Kidderminster, whimberries from the Clun Hills or asparagus, plums, celery, cucumbers and tomatoes from the Teme Valley, you can never accuse The Fruit Basket of clocking up the "food miles". Rob's customers, however, do travel a distance to buy his produce and he reckons 40% of his trade comes from visitors to the town. He notes, for example, how at Christmas people will flock from the all over the West Midlands just to buy their festive food. But the customers are clearly good fun. There is always, says Rob, the lady who will come in holding a marrow or a cucumber who asks, "have you got a bigger one?"

THE GLOBE

Our Thai restaurant has been nestled in the streets of Ludlow since 2004, during which we have won awards and praise from several areas. Chang Thai and the Globe are very much part of Ludlow life and continue to blend the local with the exotic. Thailand for most British people is a place of postcard beaches, relaxation and escapism where I have been fortunate enough to visit several times. Yet when I was asked to contribute to a book in aid of those soldiers who have seen conflict around the world I was instantly reminded of an experience in Thailand that moved me massively.

Kanchanaburi is a region of Thailand through which the renowned River Kwae runs and the Bridge over it. Actually there are historical inaccuracies in the rather Eurocentric portrayal of British heroics in the famous film. For starters the film is based on the novel, which was written about a bridge that didn't actually exist. However the "Death Railway" does cross over a tributary of the River Kwae which was renamed in 1960's Kwae Noi ('Little Kwae'). The bridge we see today was re- built from the wreckage after it was blown up at the end of the war. Anyway, pedantic inaccuracies apart,

there was a railway built by the Japanese through Thailand (Siam) to allow communications and supplies to reach the larger Japanese army in Burma. It is called the Death Railway, as about 13,000 prisoners of war from the Commonwealth, Europe and USA and 80-100,000 civilians from the region died during its making. Not far from the bridge over the "little" Kwae is a cemetery to some of those who died under appalling circumstances.

Kanchanaburi Cemetery is a beautiful place, wonderfully maintained, as is the Thai way: in the glorious exotic heat the name-plaques in polished regimentation glisten back at you. Birds sing, the scents and colours of the flowers fill the space with peacefulness, but it is the names that catch you, Smith, Malcolms and Jones etc names you can almost hear being called out in better days back in the pub in old Blighty; these young men were so far away from home, from mothers and loved ones, the glorious sun would have been alien and burdensome, the refreshing rains just more discomfort. In addition to this there are other soldiers from around the world who were also so far away from home, and this adds to the international, interconnective sadness of the cemetery. This moment did two things for me: it made me shudder with despair at the horror of war, the massive movements of people, the international disruption, the death, the pain, the crying mothers, the elderly refugees, the political conspiracies, the loneliness. This turmoil and maelstrom that can only bring sadness, there is nothing heroic about war.

Yet on a second level it made me feel a connection to these people with their familiar names, these normal people who, so far away, have died and suffered. In them there is something heroic, be it their bravery, their refusal to give in in the face of hostile odds, or those who returned who had to build new lives, be it because of disability or loss of loved ones. Normal everyday people are still in different climates around the world, a long way from a mother's hug or a partner's kiss, not knowing what the next day may bring. We should not forget these people, as we should not forget anyone, and that is why I make my small contribution to this book to help those who have been heroes far away, or face heroic personal challenges in the aftermath, when the publicity fades but they are left to rebuild their lives. I still stand inspired by the fact "That there's some corner of a foreign field that is forever England."

THE MOUSETRAP

Our business in Herefordshire started as a result of a drunken dinner with good friends of ours during the 3 counties show in Malvern. The end result was our purchase of the Mousetrap Cheese shop in Leominster & the sale of our 4 bedroom detached house in Essex! My education & early employment all revolved around agriculture, in particular dairy farming, so to be selling the end product was not that far removed as a career change. The shop in Leominster became an overnight success & we soon followed it with a similar shop in Hereford.

Our ambition had always been to make our own cheese & so the opening of our own dairy in Monkland in May 1996 was a natural progression & a good bit of "vertical integration". Our cheese "little Hereford" sold well through our own shops & so I took it out on the road selling it at Farmers markets in Birmingham, Hereford, Ledbury, Ross on Wye and also Ludlow. It

was during our second year of selling in Ludlow that i was approached by Lesley Mackley (local cook/festival organiser) to ask why we didn't have a shop in Ludlow. I politely told her that we had 3 shops plus a young family and there were only so many hours in the day! Every time we came to the market she kept asking me the same question, this carried on for a about 6 months, until she wouldn't take no for an answer and dragged me away to show me the empty shop that is 6 Church Street. The rest is history...

We are now very fortunate to have a livelihood in a part of the world we choose to live in. We have the 3 Mousetrap cheese shops in Ludlow, Leominster & Hereford all mainly selling a range of local, British & continental farmhouse cheeses, mostly made with unpasteurised milk from small dairies (like our own) that do not have the production to supply the big boys ... that is our main point of difference. We have an excellent team of staff who understand our cheeses & are able to explain their nuances to you: that is our second main point of difference!! In addition we have our own dairy at Monkland where you may come & see our little Hereford cheese being made traditionally by hand. Your visit to the dairy can be enhanced by sampling a little Hereford cheese ploughman's in our cafe, washed down with some Herefordshire cider! Plus you can take the opportunity to purchase some of our cheeses in the farm shop.

SIMPLY DELICIOUS CAKE COMPANY

O ur customers are many and varied with cakes being despatched all over the world but the greatest pleasure is sending a fruit cake to our Armed Forces in Afghanistan. As an ex soldier my self I know the importance of little home comforts and that is why we are supporting "Ludlow Food Heroes".

Home for The Simply Delicious Fruit Cake Company is amongst the gentle rolling hills of south Shropshire just a few miles from Ludlow. The fruitcakes started as an off shoot of Milly's catering business. Baked in the farmhouse kitchen and sold at various food festivals, the cakes had more appeal than weddings, parties and organizing waitresses. By 2002 the cakes were in full swing and sales began to mount up.

All the cakes are handmade to our own traditional recipes then baked in small batches so that production can be personally supervised by Milly. Each cake is packed with vine fruits, butter and of course a tot of whisky or brandy depending on the cake. Where possible we source ingredients locally – free range eggs from the farm over the hill behind us. We now bake twelve different flavours of fruitcakes in various shapes and sizes. They range from a round two inch baby fruit cake up to large family size seven inches across.

Presentation is a big thing for us too. Our cake packaging is contemporary in design and we strive for the highest standard whether the cake is eaten at home or given away as a present. All our cakes are sent out in the post in a gorgeous cream coloured gift box with our logo on the top.

The best bit is our staff - all drawn from the local rural farming community. It's a busy hard working bakery. But the cakes are made with a lot of fun and laughter too. The girls make have their own work station at which they mix by hand, bake and decorate their own batches. This gives them ownership of their cakes and a pride in what they make.

Above all this is a family business. Milly's husband Archie joined in 2005. Apart from the husband and wife team, we have mothers and daughters, father and son's, sisters, Uncle Tom Cobley and all. Archie is now responsible for running the office, marketing and product development leaving Milly to concentrate on the production and sourcing the best ingredients.

In 2008 we were very proud to be appointed by Fortnum & Mason to make their fruitcakes. Using their recipes we bake over twelve different cakes including the King George Christmas cake inspired by George IV. Our cakes reach deli's and farm shops in all corners of the country as far north to Tebay service station on the M6 and on to Scotland for The House of Bruar. Other household names we make cakes for include Harrods, Selfridges and organic cakes for Highgrove.

In 2010 our big project was introducing birthday cakes to our repertoire. Old hat but they are an everyday item and its given our web site a huge boost. Available in various sizes each cake, fruit cake or plain rich chocolate, comes in a presentation gift box with a happy birthday message printed on the icing. Customers can down load a photograph into the order form for us to make birthday card which have proved a run away success. And of course each cake comes with a candle too. Prices include next day delivery - vital if like most people you have remembered at the last minute!

And to bring it all right up to date we have produced a stunning line up of loaf cakes in eye catching packaging that last year won the best new product at the Ludlow Food Festival. As this was not enough, in 2012 we have also introduced a mini fruit cake snack bar called 'it's a piece of cake'! which is going great guns.

There is no time to put our feet up - but hopefully one day there will a chance to have a cup of tea and a slice of cake.

THE SUN INN

I was born in Blackpool, but grew up in the south of England, and when I left school in the early 70's I worked at a restaurant in a small German village near Heidelberg, before going on to study catering at Slough College. Having initially started a career in catering, it was not until many years later that I would return to working in the leisure industry. Once I left college, I proceeded to change direction and took on various sales and marketing jobs. Possibly the most enjoyable was as a director of a computer firm in the late 80's early 90's, with endless expense accounts and flash company cars etc.

However, I'm a keen sports fan and in particular football. If I had my own way and had been blessed with the talent, my chosen career would have been that of a professional footballer . My boyhood football hero George Best was a legend on and off the pitch. He was one of my early inspirations when I was a young bachelor, and other icons I admired at this time were Rod Stewart and Warren Beatty. Therefore, in my youth and on a Friday

night my pre-match ritual often consisted of copious amounts of alcohol, partying and philandering. However, I always played football to win. I guess I have carried throughout my adult life that philosophy of play hard but work hard, and my will to win has helped in my now chosen trade as landlord of the Sun.

I moved to the Shropshire/Herefordshire area in the early nineties and soon became a regular at the Sun Inn, Leintwardine, and in 2002 I moved next door to the Sun Inn. As a neighbour to former landlady Flossie Lane, I got to know her well and I'm proud that I was considered by her as not just a neighbour, but a friend.

Like a lot of her other friends and regulars of the Sun I would pop in to see her daily. Usually having a chat and making Floss a cup of tea and she would insist that I had a swift half myself.

Also as a pub regular, I would help out serving pints in the Sun, plus ordering, racking and tapping the beer. With the help of several other regulars, I organised the first beer festival at the Sun in 2006 and have continued to do so each year since. So when Flossie sadly passed away a couple of years ago, I got together with my friend Nick Davis of Hobsons Brewery, who like myself is passionate about real ale and traditional English pubs. Together we were able to take over the Sun: the rest, as they say, is history. We were keen to preserve the history of the pub, whilst putting it onto a sustainable commercial footing. A new single story eco-friendly extension at the rear of the old building has allowed us to do this. It has enabled us to offer a wider range of locally produced products, including local real ales and ciders. Therefore, as a long standing member of CAMRA (Campaign for Real Ale) I was extremely proud that the Sun Inn was awarded Herefordshire CAMRA Pub of the Year 2011, in what was our first year of trading.

With regards to Help for Heroes it is something that I feel strongly about, and with Sun Inn and it's regulars we have been able to make a small contribution to it. For instance, we have held a Sausage and Cider Festival and a Trafalgar Night Evening, both events raising money for the charity. Our Local Sea Shanty Singers, Morris Dancers and musicians gladly gave their time freely to make the events a success. We will continue to give support , with further events planned for the future.

VAUGHAN'S SANDWICH BAR

When Mark Johnson bought Ludlow's renowned "Vaughan's" sandwich bar, it was meant to be something of a stop-gap for someone with an eye for quality catering businesses. That was thirteen years ago, and though Vaughan's still retains its old name, it is Mark who stayed around to since turn it into something of a lunchtime institution in Ludlow.

Mark is one of those food perfectionists who likes to prepare all his ingredients from scratch and source as much as possible from local suppliers. In fact, 80% of all Vaughan's supplies come from just three Ludlow independents – the butcher Andrew Francis, bakery Waltons and the fruit and vegetable outlet The Fruit Basket. Almost everything that goes into Vaughan's sandwich fillings is bought fresh that day and Mark is up at 5.30 most mornings to make sure everything is up to standard.

If Vaughan's has a "signature" item it is its hot pork roast baps, complete with apple sauce, crackling and stuffing. But one must not miss the pork sausages, which are made especially for Vaughan's by Andrew Francis, and which can include meat from rare breeds including the Gloucester Old Spot, Tamworth and Berkshire Black. Mark rustles up about twenty different sandwich varieties, but he says that today are increasingly popular salad boxes, jacket potatoes, pasta and couscous.

Vaughan's fame has spread far beyond Ludlow. When the Ludlow Food festival is on during September, business for the sandwich bar rises threefold and the queues can stretch the length of King Street. Indeed, Vaughan's won the Food Festival's "Best Sandwich" competition six years in a row. The Guardian Newspaper gave Vaughan's a rave write-up and voted it the best place to eat in Ludlow "for under a tenner".

Mark is still trying to make Vaughan's even better and is experimenting with some more exotic lunchtime treats. "I only like selling what I like to eat," explains Mark. So because he likes spicy food Mark is now introducing things like Moroccan chicken, lime and chilli chicken and Italian pasta with fresh basil. Mark, of course, has to be fast. Working with his brother Paul, wife Theresa, two ladies both named Carol and another called Pam, 70% of Vaughan's daily takings come in just one-and-a-half hours over lunchtime and a sandwich can be spread and bagged in just thirty seconds!

Today Vaughan's has also introduced seating upstairs, and one can't help thinking that Mark will always want to expand and try things new. But he says he really enjoys his business and he is also delighted to be supporting Help for Heroes. "I think is it a fantastic charity," says Mark, "and I have nothing but admiration for everything it does."

WALL'S BUTCHERS

There has been a butchers on this site for a very long time – how long is uncertain. For the record, David William Wall took over the shop from a Mr. Carpenter in 1955. Wall's then moved to Craven Arms, but the shop housed two more butchers until Wall's returned about 17 years ago.

Master butcher Ian, who had joined Wall's from school, gained his promotion to manager to reopen the Ludlow branch. 10 years later, Ian became the owner.

The first thing to register with the uninitiated is the size of the shop. 'Bijou' is perhaps an understatement! The next thing would be that it is full of customers on one side of the counter, and full of butchers on the other: up to half a dozen, working shoulder to shoulder. However, customer service does not suffer. The pace and certainty of the expert staff keeps the queue moving, all the while accompanied by the buzz of recognition between servers and served. It is a miracle of logistics, helped by a shared sense of humour.

Like the other two butchers in Ludlow, the business, both retail and wholesale, is based on quality products allied to personal service. Again, most of the meat originates within a twenty mile radius of Ludlow, and from traditionally reared animals. However, there is a very specific specialisation. Ian is a long standing leading light in the 'Traditional Breeds (previously Rare Breeds) Society', which aims to encourage and extend the husbanding and consumption of old British breeds that might otherwise have disappeared in the rush to produce more meat at less cost. Beef, Ian's personal favourite, derives from breeds such as Dexter, slow-maturing but worth the wait. Pork is from free range pigs such as Gloucester Old Spot.

Wall's is also the home of 'The Ludlow Sausage'. This was a jealously guarded brand backed by a secret recipe that belonged to Carters, the last butcher in the town to close (but not for lack of trade) about five years ago. Not only did Wall's inherit the recipe and the brand, but they acquired two of Carter's butchers, as indeed did Francis's and Griffiths'. A better indication of the health of the Ludlow butchers would be hard to imagine.

A Rare Breed – The Butchers of Ludlow and The Sausage Trail

Nearly everywhere in Britain we are experiencing the decline of the traditional butcher in the face of 'convenience shopping' and scale. Many small towns have no 'proper' butchers left. Ludlow is different.

True, within not too distant memory, Ludlow, with its great food and culinary history, had over a dozen butchers. Now there are three. In alphabetical order (as they are very competitive!) We have Andrew Francis, A.Griffiths and D.W.Wall.

But this is not a last stand story – rather a chorus of "We're still standing – better than we ever were." The three are not just surviving. They are thriving and looking to the future with optimism.

The key reasons are common to all three. Firstly, the sheer depth of expertise of the men behind the counters: Literally hundreds of years of butchers' experience are shared by the twenty or so staff who will be serving customers, preparing the meat, or making sausages, pies and the rest on a normal day.

Secondly, they are customer-oriented in a way that larger enterprises can only aspire to. They meet their customers face to face every day. They recognise them, exchange local 'news' and share a laugh with them. They are part of each other's daily lives.

Crucially, they also listen, and know what the customer likes. As a result, each shop has a broad support base among Ludlow residents, some of whom swear by one specific shop, though there are many who use all three.

Last of the significant common features is the strong focus on locally sourced products. The animals are for the most part born and bred around Ludlow. They are brought up with space, sunlight, grass and individual attention. Much of the meat is from traditional British breeds, which might not produce bulk as quickly as some foreign imports, but results in better quality and taste.

If all this sounds like a 'commercial', then it's a heartfelt 'commercial' for service and quality, and for doing things the right way.

Details of the three establishments follow, for although they have much in common, they all have individual styles, different emphases and focus, and are fiercely independent, though not to the point where rivalry outweighs co-operation and shared goals.

Sausages, rich in variety and ingenuity, are a key part of each of our butcher's trade. The famous Sausage Trail, part of the Ludlow Food Festival, held each September, and an important attraction to visitors, brings the butchers into direct competition.

The format is that five businesses compete for the coveted trophies: our three resident butchers, the Ludlow Food Centre and one guest invited by the Festival Committee (note-check this!). They each prepare a special sausage, the jealously guarded recipes changing year to year. Each has a stall, and on the Saturday of the Festival a long and more or less orderly queue of sausage lovers (sausagistas?) forms from an early hour, trailing from stall to stall to taste the competition entries.

The public involved vote on pre-prepared forms to determine their favourite sausage,

This results in the award of the 'People's Choice' Trophy. Working in parallel, a panel of appointed judges votes for the other cup: 'The Experts' Choice'. Naturally, the people and the experts don't always agree......

It's an integral part of the Ludlow food story: it's hard work, it's fun, but it's also just a bit serious to our butchers!

DARK ALE AND WALNUT BREAD
FROM PRICE'S BAKERS

200g Strong white bread flour

200g Malted flour such as Bacheldre Mill's Organic Stoneground Strong Malted Blend

1 tsp salt

10g fresh yeast

30ml vegeatable oil

100g broken walnuts

230ml Ludlow Brewery's Gold Ale

1. Blend the yeast with a small amount of the ale, and leave for 10 minutes.

2. Place all the ingredients into a mixer with a dough hook attached. Mix to a soft dough and knead for 5 minutes. If mixing by hand, put the dry ingredients into a bowl and add the yeast mixture. Mix to a soft dough with the oil and ale, turn onto a floured board and knead 10 times. You may need to add more beer depending on your flour.

3. Leave for 10 minutes

4. Knead for one minute.

5. Repeat the "knead and leave" about 4 times. Let time do the work.

6. Cover and leave in a warm place for 30 minutes.

7. Give the dough a small amount of kneading to "knock back", then shape into a circle. Place onto a baking sheet and leave to prove until 1 and ½ times size. Cut a deep cross into the top of the loaf.

8. Bake at 200˚c for 30 minutes.

Smoked Sesame Seed Chocolate Truffles
From Daniel Jones Chocolatier

100g Dominican Republic Chocolate 55%

40g Double Cream

20g Sugar, Unrefined

7g Smoked Sesame Seeds, Whole

7g Smoked Sesame Seeds, Powdered

100g Dominican Republic Chocolate 55% (for dipping)

20g Sesame Seeds (for dipping)

1. **SMOKE THE SEEDS:** If using a smoker, place 30g of wood chippings (preferably oak) under the base tray, cover with lid and allow smoke to build up over a gently heat. If using a frying pan, place a piece of foil into the dry pan, followed by 30g of wood chippings. Cover with a second piece of foil and cover with a second frying (upside down). Allow smoke to build up over a gently heat. Once there is a sign of smoke add all of the required sesame seeds (14g). Cover, remove from heat source and allow to smoke for 4-5 mins, taking care not to burn the seeds. Remove from heat and allow to cool. Keep half as whole seeds and turn the other half into a fine powder using a pestle and morter.

2. **GANACHE:** Place the cream and sugar into a stainless steel sauté pan. Heat gently for 4 mins or until a temperature of 60°C is reached. Do not allow to boil. Remove from heat.

3. Meanwhile, melt 100g of chocolate over a bain marie to a temperature of 49°C. Do not allow to get too hot. Pour the slightly cooled cream over the melted chocolate and stir with a rubber spatula until smooth and glossy. Add the

smoked sesame seeds and powdered seeds. Pour into a plastic tray and leave in the fridge for one hour, or until firm.

4. **ROLL THE TRUFFLES:** Roll the truffles between the palms of your hands and place on a tray lined with a silicone mat or baking paper. Return to the fridge to firm up.

5. **TEMPERING:** Melt the two thirds of the remaining chocolate over a bain marie to a temperature of 49°C. Stir in the remaining third and stir until fully melted. This will reduce the chocolate to a 'working' temperature of 31°C and allow for a crisp snap and clean sheen.

6. **TO FINISH:** Using a fork, dip each rolled truffle into the tempered chocolate and then roll in the remaining sesame seeds (optional). Leave to set fully on a baking sheet, lined with a silicone mat or baking paper, for at least 1 hour.

7. Store in an airtight container at room temperature and consumer within two weeks.

PAVLOVA RECIPE FOR WOOD BURNING COOKERS
From Ludlow Stoves

This is one of my favourite recipes and looks really impressive served at a dinner party or BBQ. It is so simple, and you really don't need to use vinegar or cornflour. The key is to be able to hold the bowl above your head! You can either make one large Pavlova or lots of small meringues and glue them together with cream.

3 large eggs

6 oz (175g) caster sugar

For the topping;

10fl oz (275 ml) double cream

Any mixed berries, I love raspberries, strawberries and blackcurrants. Pineapple, kiwi fruit and passion fruit are also a lovely alternative.

1. Place the egg whites in a large clean bowl and have the sugar measured and ready. Now whisk the egg whites until they form soft peaks and you can turn the bowl upside down without them sliding out (it's very important, though, not to over-whisk the egg whites because, if you do, they will start to collapse).

2. When they're ready, raise the temperature of the oven in your wood burning stove to 150°C. Start to whisk in the sugar, approximately 1 oz (25 g) at a time, whisking after each addition until all the sugar is in. Now take a metal tablespoon and spoon the meringue mixture on to the prepared baking sheet, forming a circle about 8 inches (20 cm) in diameter. Spoon round blobs next to each other so that they join up

to form a circle all around the edge. Now, using the tip of a skewer, make little swirls in the meringue all around the edge, lifting the skewer up sharply each time to leave tiny peaks. Now place the baking sheet in the oven, then let some heat out the oven and lower and lower the temperature slightly to 140°C and leave it to cook for 1 hour. Check to see that it is totally cooked through. Remember to keep an eye on the pavlova to ensure it does not burn.

3. I then move the Pavlova to the warming compartment under the oven until it's completely cold. I always find it's best to make a Pavlova in the evening and leave it overnight to dry out, and leave the fire to go out too. This isn't necessary but it does make it lovely and sticky in the middle. You can serve immediately once cold.

4. To serve the Pavlova, lift it from the baking sheet, peel off the paper and place it on a serving dish. Then just before serving, spread the whipped cream on top, arrange the fruit on top of the cream and dust with a little sifted icing sugar. Serve cut into wedges.